All The Words Unsaid

Haley Schaefer

Presentation by *BookLeaf Publishing*

Web: www.bookleafpub.com

E-mail: info@bookleafpub.com

ISBN: 9789357742320

First edition 2023

*To myself, for finding strength and courage
to speak when it felt impossible, so I wrote.*

*As well, to my grandparents who chose to
raise me when the people who were created
to, did not see fit and chose not to, stemmed
from their selfishness.*

*I would never be the person I am today had
I not known their love, even when they did
not have to make the sacrifices they did.*

ACKNOWLEDGEMENT

To every person who has entered and made an impact on my life thus far.
Positive or negative.

PREFACE

This book came into being simply from an idea. An idea that maybe it can be hard to understand thoughts intertwined with a million feelings at once. So, creating a collection of writings from my personal experience with understanding this concept, has blossomed into this book you are about to read. Sometimes, speaking and understanding feelings from wounds, new or old, is near impossible. This book has allowed the impossible to become possible.

Ashes

To think, all this time I was loving a memory.

Growing Pains

The hurt consumes you,
until you realize it does not define you.
It never has.
That is growth.

Astrophile

You are like the moon and stars.
Lighting up the galaxy in the midst of such
immense darkness.
And bringing such beauty into something so
unknown.
Love.

A Gentle Soul

It takes such a grace,
to continue forward in kindness
even in the midst of chaos and hurt.

Journey

5

Travel. See the world you were created in, and learn to love it. Love where you are, in any aspect.
It is hard to love when you are unhappy with your surroundings.

Who Is Vienna?

"Vienna waits for you!"
Paradise waits?
Success waits?
A life created on your own cannot wait for you.
It is up to you to create it. To pursue it. To dig
deep and find what you want to encapsulate the
fabrics of what has and will be created.
It is impossible to be satisfied with a life you do
not allow yourself to love that you created for
just YOU.

Creation

It is such a gift to live in this world,
most simply just exist.

Inner Monologue

I lay awake at night and my mind whirs for
hours. I cannot make it stop.
"Should I have done this differently?"
"What would have happened if I said this
instead?" "How could I have been better?" "Will
I ever be enough? Could I ever be enough, for
myself?"
They are endless.
But the reality is, each day has an end.
Each day is a new chance to better yourself, but
not for the sake of being accepted by a stranger.
Self-reflect, but do not let inner insecurities alter
how you uphold yourself for the sake of others.
At the end of each day, you only have yourself.
Prioritize you, over anyone or anything else.

Misapprehensions

9

"It was hard." I exclaimed.
"But not as hard as realizing what I was holding
onto, was no longer mine."
I nodded to myself with acceptance.

Crawling My Way Back Up

Sometimes you have to hit that point of rock bottom. That feeling of nothing, but everything at once.
Allowing it to alter your understanding of where you are and where you want to be.
Then, you can only go up.

Your Own

Be, but be as you have strived to become, and be nothing less.

Achilles

The delusion that one is inevitably whole. No
hero has ever been whole, no matter the battles
of triumph only documented.
Every person has some darkness to them.
Embrace and love that part of you too.

Alchemy

13

You are divinely mine, and always have been.

Muse

An ode to be part of the poem,
and not always the poet.

Longing

I long for a place that is not physical. A place
that is a feeling.
A feeling of being, and feeling free.

Being Understood

"You speak through film,"
"and that is something I admire about you."
My soul felt loved in that moment.
Until I realized it was something I made up.

Eyes

"The eyes are the gateway to the soul," they say. I did not believe it until I saw the life slowly drain from your eyes, until you were lifeless in my arms.

Get Up

No one is coming to save you.
Only yourself.